Spiders

Preschool/Kindergarten

Save time and energy planning thematic units with this comprehensive resource. We've searched the 1991–1997 issues of **The MAILBOX**® and **Teacher's Helper**® magazines to find the best ideas for you to use when teaching a thematic unit on spiders. Included in this book are favorite units from the magazines, single ideas to extend a unit, and a variety of reproducible activities. Pick and choose from these activities to develop your own complete unit or to simply enhance your current lesson plans. You're sure to find everything you need right here in this book to spin a creative and integrated web of learning.

Editors:
Michele M. Dare
Angie Kutzer
Allison E. Ward

Artist:
Jennifer L. Tipton

Cover Artist:
Jennifer L. Tipton

Visit Our Web Site At www.themailbox.com

©1999 by THE EDUCATION CENTER, INC.
All rights reserved.
ISBN# 1-56234-291-6

Manufactured in the United States
10 9 8 7 6 5 4 3 2 1

Table Of Contents

Thematic Units...

from The MAILBOX® magazine.

Itsy-bitsy
& Other Spider Friend

Spiders, as creepy as they sometimes seem, are helpful and amazing creatures. Use the songs, reproducible spider booklet, bulletin board, circle game, spider pendant, and even a web cake to lure your little ones into a web woven of wonder.

ideas by Lucia Kemp Henry

Up Close And Personal

Find a house spider or garden spider for youngsters to observe for several days in your classroom. Provide your spider guest with a large screen-topped glass jar accessorized with leafy shrub branches and a damp sponge piece. Feed the spider two flies or mealworms a week. Lightly mist the habitat with a plant mister once a week. Encourage youngsters to describe the activities of the spider.

Read All About It

Spiders are not so scary when students know the facts about these members of the arachnid family. Give your youngsters some background information with an excellent book called *Eyewitness Juniors Amazing Spiders* by Alexandra Parsons. In this book, each two-page spread contains a large picture of a spider surrounded by brief text containing fascinating facts. Share the pictures, and read and discuss some of the facts to pique your youngsters' interests and to demystify these eight-legged creatures.

"Spider-rific" Headbands

The spiders on these headbands aren't itsy-bitsy at all. But they can be a lot of fun, especially when worn to perform the poem/song "Ten Little Spiders." To make a spider headband cut a paper strip the correct length for a headband, and glue or staple it. Accordion-fold eight construction-paper strips (3/4" x 12") and glue four to each side of the headband. Glue on a 3 1/2-inch paper circle, and decorate it with large wiggle eyes and dimensional paint.

Miss Muffet, who lived about 200 years ago, was the daughter of an English doctor. Her dad probably kept spiders to be ground up and used as a treatment for a fever or cold.

For real?

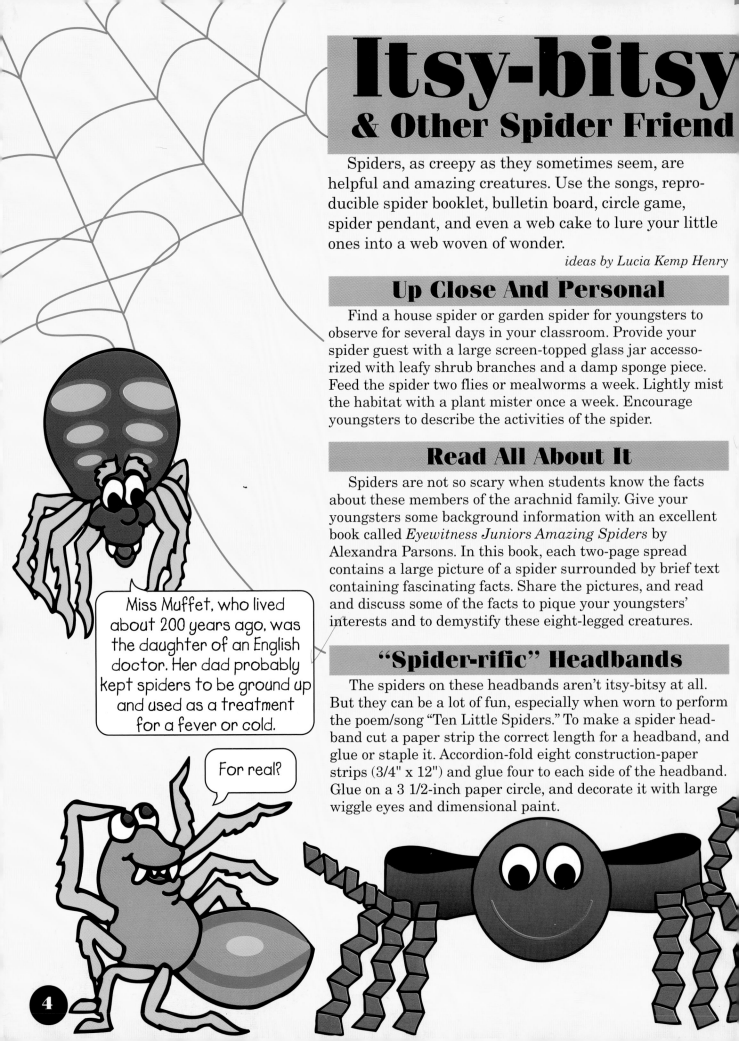

Spiders On The Move

Get your youngsters moving with this active poem/song. And, by all means, have them wear their spider headbands for the performance.

Ten Little Spiders
(sung to the tune of "Ten Little Indians")

One spider up and two spiders down.
Three spiders turn around and 'round.
Four spiders smile, and then they frown.
Oh, what a wonderful sight!

Come up on tiptoes. Squat down.
Turn around slowly.
Smile and frown.
Rock head from side to side.

Five spiders in and six spiders out.

Move wiggling fingers into and out of a cupped hand.

Seven spiders spin around about.
Eight spiders climb the waterspout.
Oh, what a wonderful sight!

Spin around quickly.
Pretend to climb.
Rock head from side to side.

Nine spiders each have eight little legs.
Ten spiders lay little spider eggs.
All spiders wiggle their little legs.
Oh, what a wonderful sight!

Hold up and wiggle eight fingers.
Make egg shape with fingers.
Wiggle legs.
Rock head from side to side.

by Lucia Kemp Henry

Make-And-Take Booklet

When students make these spider booklets, they are sure to share what they've learned with friends and family. Reproduce the booklet cover (page 10) onto construction paper. Mount the construction paper on tagboard and cut out the octagonal shape. Trace the web with dimensional glitter paint, Elmer's® GluColors™, or a paint pen. (Depending on the fine-motor skills of your students, you may want to have parent volunteers prepare the webs in advance.) To place a spider in the web, begin by gluing eight 2 1/2-inch pipe-cleaner legs around the spider body outline. Glue a 1 1/2-inch pom-pom to the cover for the spider's body; then attach a 1-inch pom-pom for the spider's head.

Reproduce the booklet pages (pages 11–14) on white construction paper. For each page in turn, read, discuss, and complete it as directed. Then cut out each booklet page, and staple the pages in order beneath the booklet cover.

There are billions of us. We help keep the insect population under control.

The Spider Spins A Web

Youngsters can create a web of their own while playing this cooperative singing game. Seat your youngsters in a circle, spaced about one foot apart. Supply a large ball of loosely wound yarn. As they sing "The Spider Spins A Web" (page 6), have youngsters roll the yarn ball across the floor to one another. When the yarn ball comes to a student, he grasps the yarn strand, holds it against the floor, and rolls the yarn ball to someone who hasn't yet had it. (Stress that each child must continue holding his strand of yarn to the floor, or the web will break.) When each student is holding the yarn, a weblike tangle of yarn will have been created. Ask students to carefully let go of their yarn strands and stand up to view their web-making expertise!

We spiders have a reputation for being vicious and scary. But most of us are helpful rather than harmful to people.

The Spider Spins A Web

(sung to the tune of "The Farmer In The Dell")

The spider spins a web.
The spider spins a web.
Round, round, up and down,
The spider spins a web.

Additional Verses:
She spins it in and out.
She spins it back and forth.
She spins it good and strong.

Special Spider Pendants

Spiders may become very popular with your students when they get to assemble and wear these spider pendants. To begin a spider pendant, press a 1-inch Styrofoam® ball and a 1 1/2-inch Styrofoam® ball against a tabletop. Position the balls with the flattened sections together. Poke a bamboo meat skewer through both balls. (For safety reasons, you will probably want to complete this step for each child.) Wrap the exposed pointed skewer end with tape for safety. Put craft glue where the flattened Styrofoam® surfaces touch, and allow the glue to dry overnight. Spray the balls with acrylic paint. When the paint has dried, use a marker to add eyes. Remove the tape from the meat skewer, and carefully remove the skewer from the balls.

To complete the project, thread a 36-inch length of yarn on a large plastic needle. Knot the ends. Using the threaded needle, insert the yarn into the larger ball and pull it through. Repeatedly knot the yarn beneath the larger ball until the knot is of sufficient size to hold the yarn in place. Cut the yarn just below the needle and tie the yarn ends to form a necklace. Use a skewer to poke four holes through the larger ball. (To be on the safe side, do this for each child.) Push one 4-inch piece of pipe cleaner through each hole and center it. Bend the pipe cleaner to resemble spider legs.

Accentuating The Positive

Reinforce the positive aspects of the arachnid family with this upbeat spider song.

Spider, Spider

(sung to the tune of "Daisy, Daisy")

Spider, Spider, you are a friend, I know.
You eat bugs that eat little plants that grow.
You really are not so scary. You're not so very hairy.
You have eight feet. Your web is neat. Little spidery friend of mine.

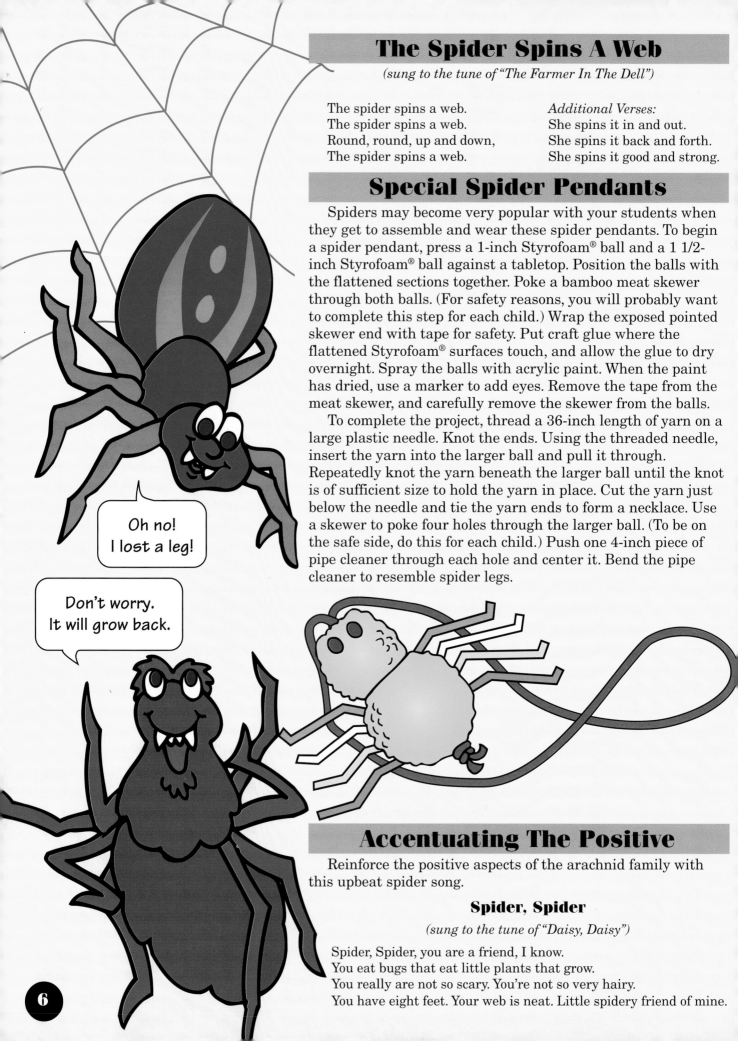

Oh no!
I lost a leg!

Don't worry.
It will grow back.

Step Into Our Center

If you want to add to the spidery effect of this visual discrimination exercise for your centers, decorate the area with a few store-bought cobwebs (available before Halloween). Then duplicate the patterns on pages 8 and 9 onto tagboard. Laminate and cut out the pieces. To use the center, a student places the three spider bodies on a tabletop and arranges the eight matching legs with each body.

Itsy-bitsy's Web Of Friends

This spidery bulletin-board web will provide a colorful and cheerful backdrop. To prepare a bulletin board, first cover it with dark blue bulletin-board paper. Use a pencil or chalk to lightly sketch a web shape to cover the entire board. Trace over the web with white oil pastel, crayon, or paint. Add the title "Spectacular Spiders" to the board.

Have each youngster prepare a spider to add to this giant web. To make a spider, begin with a three-inch and a two-inch Styrofoam® ball half. Press each ball half against a tabletop, creating a flattened surface. To create a spider body, use craft glue to glue the ball halves together along the flattened sections, and allow the glue to dry overnight. A large rubber band may be used to hold the pieces in place. Spray paint the spider body any color except blue. When the paint has dried, attach eyes and three-inch pipe-cleaner lengths for legs. Add the finishing touches with dimensional paint and allow the spider to dry. Pin each spider to the bulletin-board web.

Reading Web

The following books are excellent literature tie-ins to use during your spider unit: *The Very Busy Spider* by Eric Carle, *Anansi And The Moss-covered Rock* by Eric A. Kimmel, and *Anansi The Spider: A Tale From The Ashanti* retold by Gerald McDermott.

Spider Web Cakes

This yummy spider surprise is sure to be a hit! Prepare your favorite cake mix in round pans according to the package directions, but do not stack the layers. Frost each layer separately with white frosting to make two cakes. With chocolate frosting, make four concentric circles on each cake layer. Starting at the center of each cake, pull a knife to the outer edge. Repeat this seven times to create a weblike look. Put a spider on each web. Clean plastic spiders can be used. Or make your own spiders by sticking licorice lace lengths in the sides of gumdrops.

I'm off!

Using his silk threads as a parachute, he can ride a breeze for hundreds of miles. Far-out!

Spider Body Patterns

Use with "Step Into Our Center" on page 7.

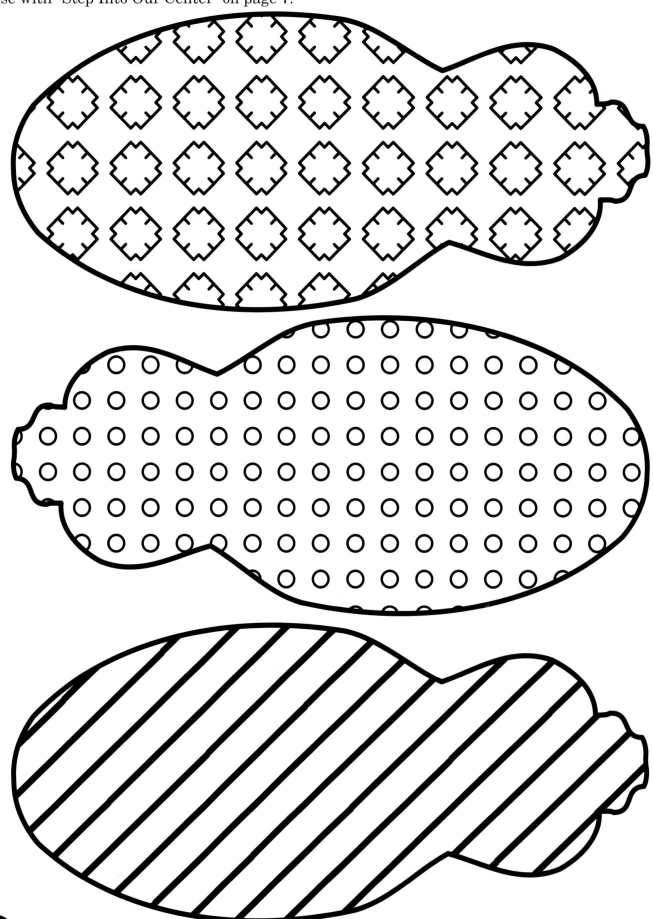

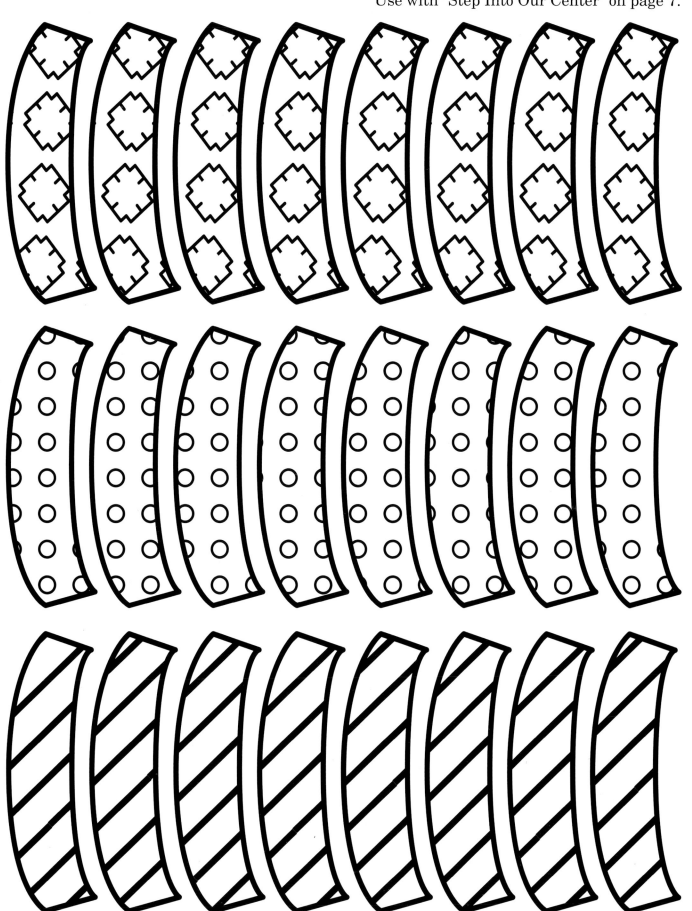

Spider Booklet Cover

Use with "Make-And-Take Booklet" on page 5.

SPIDERS

by

©The Education Center, Inc.

Color the spider **yellow.**

Cut.

Glue.

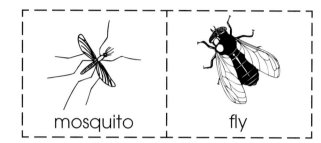

mosquito | fly

1

Spiders eat insect pests.

Spider Booklet

Use with "Make-And-Take Booklet" on page 5.

Color the spider **brown.**

Cut.

Glue.

8

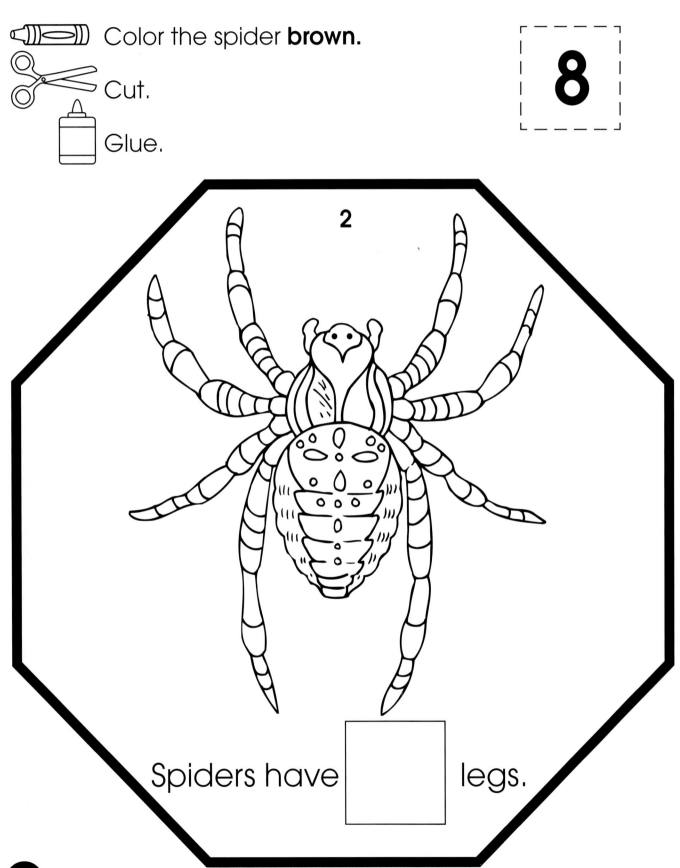

2

Spiders have ☐ legs.

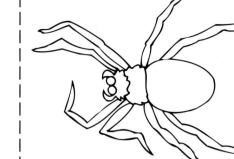

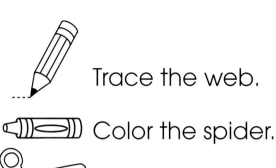 Trace the web.

Color the spider.

Cut.

Glue.

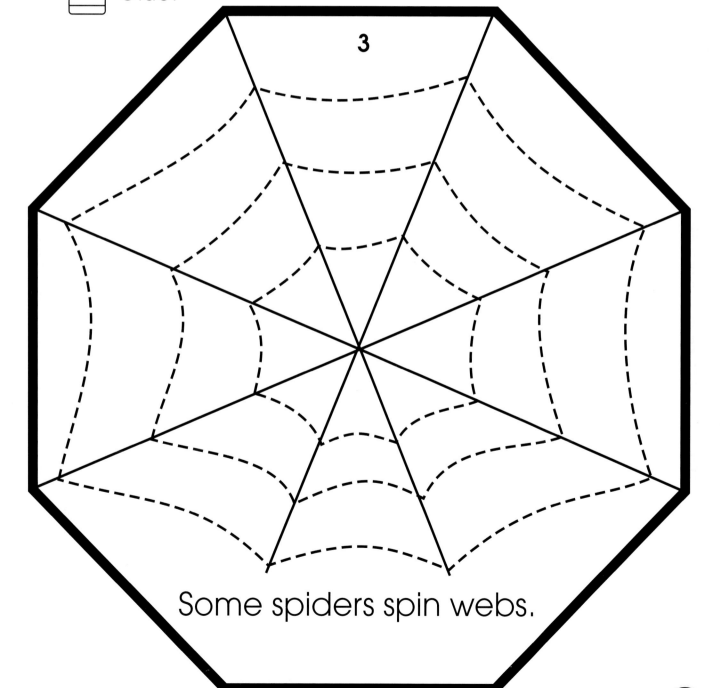

3

Some spiders spin webs.

Spider Booklet

Use with "Make-And-Take Booklet" on page 5.

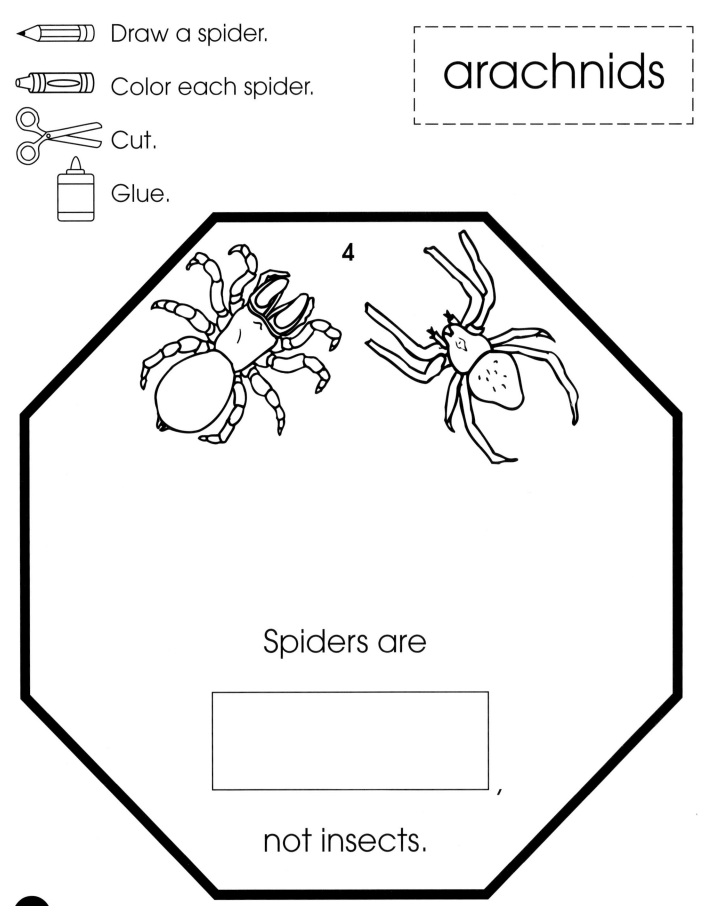

Draw a spider.

Color each spider.

Cut.

Glue.

arachnids

4

Spiders are

not insects.

Miss Muffet Goes Modern

Are you familiar with Miss Muffet, her tuffet, and the spider that frightened her away? Use the ideas in this unit to learn about the *new* Miss Muffet and her colorful arachnid friends.

ideas contributed by Lucia Kemp Henry

Little Miss Muffet sat on a tuffet,
Eating her cookies three.
Along came a spider
Who sat down beside her,
And stayed with Miss Muffet for tea!

Out With The Old, In With The New

Recite the familiar rhyme describing Miss Muffet's upsetting encounter. Then recite the updated rhyme above. Ask youngsters to compare and contrast the attitude and circumstances of the two tuffet sitters. Then take a poll. Which Miss Muffet would they rather be?

Miss Muffet's Not The Only One...

According to David Kirk's *Miss Spider's Tea Party* (Scholastic Inc.), Miss Muffet's not the only one with a fear of spiders. Read aloud this story that stars a friendly spider who invites her insect neighbors to a tea party. Your little ones will be as delighted as the insect guests with Miss Spider's graciousness. Follow up the story by having students make these spider cookies. Then seat youngsters on their tuffets and serve the cookies with some tea.

Spider Cookies

Use a permanent marker to personalize a foil square for each child. Place a 1/4-inch-thick slice of refrigerated cookie dough on each child's square. Direct each child to break four pretzel sticks in half and press eight halves into opposite sides of the slice. Have each child then press two M&M's® brand mini baking bits into his slice to resemble eyes. Place the children's foil squares and cookies on a tray; then bake the cookies according to package directions.

Oh, Miss Muffet; oh, Miss Muffet;
Oh, hello! How do you do?
I'm a small and friendly spider.
May I sit down here with you?

Little spider, little spider,
Oh, hello! How do you do?
You're a small and friendly spider.
Sit **beside** me, please won't you?

Finger Friends

Unlike the original Miss Muffet, your little ones may become fond of spiders when they make these friendly finger puppets. For each child, use a kitchen knife to press a finger-sized hole into a two-inch Styrofoam® ball. Have each child use tempera paint to paint the ball the color of his choice. When the paint is dry, have him press eight pipe-cleaner legs into the ball and glue on wiggle eyes. Press a small piece of masking tape labeled with the child's initials onto the bottom of the spider. Invite youngsters to use their puppets while singing the above song to the tune of "Clementine." Repeat the song, substituting *beside* with *above*, *below*, and *behind*.

Glue

More Finger Fun

The finger fun continues with this booklet project. Duplicate a tuffet pattern (on page 18) onto the top and bottom half of each of two sheets of paper. Program each half with a position word (*beside, on, above,* or *below*). Duplicate a class supply of the programmed pages; then cut them in half. Give each child a set of pages stapled together between a cover, if desired. To complete his booklet, a child presses a fingerprint onto the page so that the print's position corresponds to the word on that page. He then uses a marker to add legs and features to each spider.

Miss M's Spider Game

Here's a game that the modern Miss Muffet would proudly endorse. To prepare a game for two players, duplicate a pair of spider patterns and a pair of tuffet patterns (on page 18) onto four colors of construction paper. Cut out the patterns. Prepare a spinner displaying the four colors. To begin play, each child is given one of each color of spider and tuffet to arrange in rows in front of him. In turn each child spins the spinner, then places that color of spider on or removes it from its matching tuffet. Play continues until a player's four spiders are seated on matching tuffets.

Miss Muffet's Math Manipulatives

Not only does the modern Miss Muffet invite spiders to stay for tea; she also invites them to participate in math fun. If you think your little ones would enjoy math Miss Muffet's way, duplicate multiple sets of the spider patterns (on page 18) onto various colors of construction paper. Cut out the patterns. Draw several large webs on poster board, adding glittery touches to the webs if desired. Working with a small group, use the spiders and webs for all sorts of classification and counting fun.

Get Caught Learning!

Invite parents to get caught having fun with their children when you send home these learning games. For each child, duplicate copies of the spider patterns on page 18 onto several colors of paper; then cut them out. Have each child color a copy of the Miss Muffet pattern and parent note (on page 19). Glue the pattern onto a paper lunch bag; then personalize the bag. Send the bag home with the parent note and spiders tucked inside.

Patterns

Use with "More Finger Fun" on page 16, and "Miss M's Spider Game," "Miss Muffet's Math Manipulatives," and "Get Caught Learning!" on page 17.

Dear Parent,

No need to fear when these spiders are near! They're here for all sorts of math fun! Recite the traditional Miss Muffet rhyme with your child. Then recite the updated rhyme about the modern Miss Muffet. For fun, sort Miss Muffet's arachnid friends by color. Or make patterns using two colors of spiders. Miss Muffet and her spiders hope you get caught in a web of learning fun!

Little Miss Muffet sat on a tuffet,
Eating her curds and whey.
Along came a spider
Who sat down beside her,
And frightened Miss Muffet away!

Little Miss Muffet sat on a tuffet,
Eating her cookies three.
Along came a spider
Who sat down beside her,
And stayed with Miss Muffet for tea!

©The Education Center, Inc. • *Spiders* • Preschool/Kindergarten • TEC3189

Little Miss Muffet

More Ideas For

Spidery Sensation

What's black and white and creeping with spiders? The contents of your sensory table when you fill it with black and white shredded paper (available at party-supply stores) and a quantity of plastic spiders. Encourage a child to find the spiders, then count them. Your little ones are sure to love this sensory-table surprise!

Susan Burbridge—Four-Year-Olds
Colonial Hills United Methodist School
San Antonio, TX

Spunky Spinning Spiders

Mary
Juan
Jaye
Kate
Tim
Dave
Jessie
Stevie
Karim
Keiko

Spin a splendid display by stapling a yarn web onto a background. Then add spunky student-made spiders. To make one, glue together one large and one smaller paper circle. Add cut-out eyes accented with black marker; then glue on accordion-folded paper legs.

Barbara Meyers
Fort Worth Country Day School
Fort Worth TX

Your Web ●●●●●●●●●●

Egg-Cup Spiders

Spin a web of fun with egg-cup spiders. In advance, cut apart the egg cups from several cardboard egg cartons. Poke four holes in each of two sides of each cup. Have each youngster paint the inside and outside of his cup with black tempera. When his cup is dry, have him insert a black pipe-cleaner length into each hole and then bend each length inside the cup to hold it in place. To complete the project, have youngsters glue on tiny wiggle eyes. These spiders look especially spiffy suspended from the classroom ceiling!

Melanie Rand—Gr. K, Camey Elementary, The Colony, TX

Spider Climbing

Have your itsy-bitsy spiders try this fun gross-motor activity. In advance cut a large insect pattern from tagboard. Punch a hole in the pattern and use a piece of yarn to tie it to the top of a playground play dome or net climber. Then have your little ones pretend that the dome or net climber is a spiderweb and that they are spiders. In turn, have each child climb the dome or net—imagining that it is a sticky web—to reach the insect.

adapted from an idea by Lori Kracoff, Thornton, NH

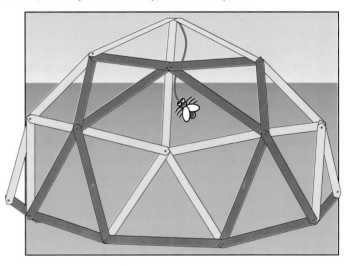

Spider Wear

Creepy crawlers will be popping up all over when you make these spider hats. Measure and cut a black tagboard strip to fit around each child's head. Staple the ends of the strip together to make a headband. Have each child cut eight strips of black construction paper, then accordion-fold each strip. Staple four of the strips to one side of the headband and four strips to the other. Now your little ones are ready for spider wear!

Cathy Gust—Gr. K
Stiegel Elementary School
Manheim, PA

Webbed Feat

Your youngsters can make their own tactile spiderwebs similar to those in *The Very Busy Spider*, by Eric Carle. Have each student begin by drawing a spider in one corner of a white piece of paper. Then, in step-by-step fashion, demonstrate how to use a squeeze glue bottle to create lines of glue that resemble an asterisk. Atop his asterisk, have each student make concentric glue circles. When the glue is dry, your youngsters will have delightfully tactile webs. As a variation of this activity, make glue webs on black paper or use Elmer's® GluColors™ (decorative color glue).

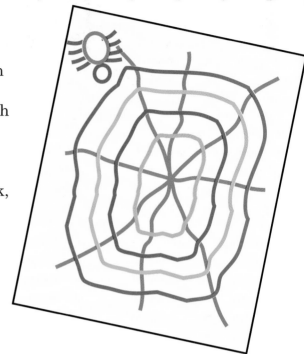

Alex

Hiss, hiss!
Want to slither in the grass?

The Very Busy Spider: On Location

Have your youngsters decide on a new location for the very busy spider. Once a location (such as a zoo, circus, jungle, or desert) has been decided upon, have each youngster specify a creature found in that location. Then have him glue a tissue-paper representation of this creature on white art paper along with a glue or glue-and-glitter web. As the student dictates, write a sentence including a sound the creature would make and a question for the spider. For example: "Hiss, hiss!" said the snake. "Want to slither in the grass?" Join these pages with metal rings for lots of reading fun!

Spiders In Your Tummy

After your youngsters have had the pleasure of hearing *The Very Busy Spider*, tempt their taste buds with spider snacks! Have each youngster spread cream cheese (tinted, if desired) between two round crackers, before inserting eight pretzel "legs" into the cheese. Youngsters complete the creepy-crawly effect by attaching two raisin "eyes" atop the cracker body using cream cheese. As students munch this "spider-rific" snack, play "Spider On The Floor" from Raffi's *Singable Songs For The Very Young*.

Catch That Fly!

Just as the early bird gets the worm, the hardworking spider gets the fly in the classroom favorite, *The Very Busy Spider*, by Eric Carle (Philomel Books). Tape a plastic fly or a cut-out picture of a fly to one end of a large ball of yarn. Wrap the yarn around the fly so that the fly is hidden in the ball of yarn. Share the story; then have students practice the animal sounds mentioned in the book. Arrange the group in a circle; then lead them in working together to spin a web in order to catch a fly of their own. To begin, hold the end of the yarn, name a farm animal, and make that animal's sound. Then roll the ball of yarn to a child in the circle. Direct that child to repeat the procedure of holding, naming, sounding, and rolling. Continue until the ball of yarn is unwound, a web is formed, and the fly is "caught." You'll have some very busy children during this follow-up activity!

Dawn Hurley, CUMC Child Care Center,
Bethel Park, PA

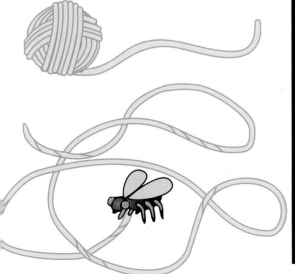

Itsy-Bitsy Puppet

Make a puppet to use while singing the favorite song "The Itsy-Bitsy Spider." From felt, cut a sun shape and a cloud shape small enough to fit inside a paper cup. Glue the shapes, back-to-back, on one end of a pipe cleaner. Wrap one end of a second pipe cleaner around a plastic spider that is also small enough to fit inside the cup. Punch two small holes in the bottom of the paper cup. Insert the pipe cleaners through the holes so that the shapes and the spider are hidden inside the cup. As you sing, slide the pipe cleaners up and down, revealing the corresponding shapes. Youngsters will want to sing the song over and over again when moving their very own itsy-bitsy spider puppets.

Karen Naylor—Pre-K
Palmer Preschool
Salem, NH

Book Note
Use with "Catch That Fly!"

We were very busy today!
After reading
The Very Busy Spider
by Eric Carle,

we spun a class web
and caught a fly!

Let's go outside and search for spiderwebs!

Little Miss Muffet's Spider Count

Your youngsters will have lots of creepy counting fun as they prepare these individual counting booklets. Fold four sheets of paper in half and staple them to create an eight-page booklet. Decorate the cover, add a title, and write your name. Open the booklet and number each page sequentially. Starting with page one, make a set of spiders to match the number. To make a spider's body, press your thumb onto a black ink pad and then onto the booklet page. Use a fine-tip marker to add legs and other details to the fingerprint body. When this booklet is complete, everyone can have a good laugh as they flip the pages counting spiders and improving their math skills.

Susan Puckett—Gr. K
Pearl Lower Elementary, Pearl, MS

In And Out Of The Web

Although this is a game Little Miss Muffet would have shied away from, your little ones are likely to be drawn to it like bugs to a web. Make a spinner gameboard similar to the one shown. For spiderwebs, glue a real berry basket near each corner. Each player is given four spider rings to start play. In turn, each child spins and puts a spider in his basket or takes one out of his basket as directed by the spinner. Play continues until one player has all four of his spiders in his basket.

Jane Nash—Gr.K
Pearl Lower Elementary
Pearl, MS

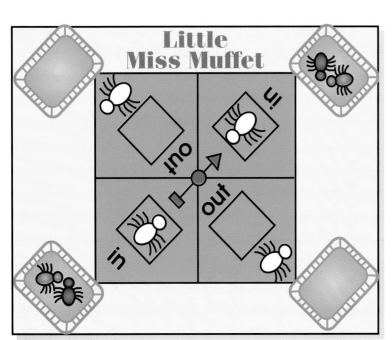

Splat! It's A Spider!

Paint a child's palm and four fingers with black paint. Have her press her hand onto a sheet of construction paper twice so that the palm prints overlap and the finger prints extend in opposite directions. When the paint is dry, glue on colorful wiggle eyes. Even Miss Muffet would invite this spider to sit down beside her!

Kathy Folz, South Elementary, Franklin Park, IL

Spider Eights

Using a die-cutter machine, cut out a numeral eight for each child. Direct him to glue eight pipe-cleaner legs onto his spider. Then provide a variey of craft supplies for each child to use to decorate his spider as he likes. Display the finished creatures crawling around your classroom walls.

J. Davy, Dozier Elementary, Erath, LA

Webs Of Delight

Plastic spiders and yards of yarn transform paper plates into convincing spiderwebs. To make a web, begin by snipping slits at equal intervals around a seven-inch black paper plate. Knot a length of yarn. Insert the yarn in a slit so that the knot is to the back of and up against the plate. Then pull the yarn tautly across the plate, securing it in a slit on the opposite side. Pull the yarn tautly across the back of the plate and up through a different slit. Continue "weaving" the web in this manner until the yarn has nearly run out. Slip a plastic spider ring onto the yarn before pulling the yarn through one final slit. Knot the yarn on the back of the plate.

Diane Bonica—Preschool
Living Savior Preschool, Tualatin, OR

Creepy-Crawly Color Game

Use some paper spiders and their web to create a color-matching activity. First make a playing board by cutting a six-sided, spiderweb shape from white poster board. Draw lines to divide the web into six equal-sized, pie-shaped sections. Color each section a different color; then print the corresponding color word on the outer edge of each section. Cut six spiders from black construction paper; then hole-punch a pair of eyes for each spider that corresponds to a color on the playing board. Glue a pair of eyes to each spider. Finish assembling the game by affixing one piece of adhesive magnetic tape to each section of the playing board and one to the back of each spider. To play, a child matches each spider's eye color to the corresponding color on the web playing board.

Niki Huff—Pre-K
Stilwell United Methodist Preschool
Stilwell, KS

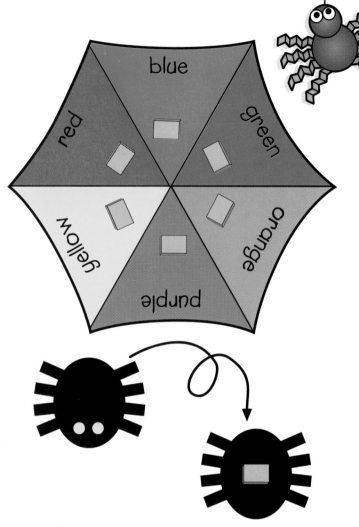

Spider Party Bags

This little tote, with a creepy-crawly look, will come in handy at the end of your spider unit. To make one, draw portions of a spider-web in one corner of a white or brown lunch bag. Sponge-paint two black circles on the bag. While the paint is still wet, sprinkle a few specks of glitter onto each circle. When it's dry, attach hole reinforcements for the eyes. With a marker draw legs on each spider. Fill the tote with a spidery treat, then fold the top of the bag down, punch two holes, and tie a length of curling ribbon through the holes.

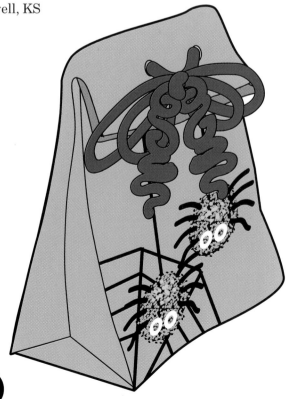

Pat Gaddis—Pre-K
St. Timothy's Methodist Church School
Houston, TX

Reproducible Activities...

......Miss Spider's Tea Party......

Note To The Teacher

This unit has been designed to be used with *Miss Spider's Tea Party,* written and illustrated by David Kirk. This story can serve as an excellent springboard to introduce the Itsy-Bitsies/Visual Discrimination unit and the Spider Pop-Up Booklet.

From MISS SPIDER'S TEA PARTY by David Kirk. Copyright ©1994 by Callaway Editions, Inc. Reprinted by permission of Scholastic, Inc.

Background For The Teacher
David Kirk
Author Of Miss Spider's Tea Party

As a toymaker, David Kirk dreamed up thousands of characters before he even started to paint picture books. Prior to his remarkable success in the world of children's publishing, Kirk was the founder and designer of two toy companies, Ovicular Toyworks and Hoobert Toys, where he made everything from bright, three-dimensional wooden alligators to multicolored robots influenced by his boyhood toy collection. Each toy was distinguished by its unique design, and each was packed in a little box with a painting on the outside. Kirk's indulgence in the detail and color of his toys caught the attention of book packager Nicholas Callaway, who encouraged Kirk to consider painting a children's book.

Then along came a spider: Miss Spider. Inspired by his daughter Violet's love for insects in the family garden, Kirk found the perfect subject for his story: bugs. *Miss Spider's Tea Party*, a lush counting book with mesmerizing oil-on-paper illustrations, quickly became a phenomenon, landing on national bestseller lists and earning praise from booksellers and librarians across the country. Children (and adults) instantly fell in love with the eight-legged beauty named Miss Spider. Kirk then followed up his success with a second bug tale told in verse, *Miss Spider's Wedding*, the rhyming story of how his flower-eating arachnid finds her perfect spider man.

Kirk had studied painting for more than 20 years, starting in junior high school. A graduate of Cleveland Art Institute, his bold palette and unique style are influenced by everything from nineteenth-century academic painting to 1930's animation. But it was an unusual volume, which Kirk discovered in the back of an old bookshop, that directly influenced his style on the Miss Spider books.

"I found a small copy of *The Gnomes Almanac* by little-known Viennese author Ida Bohtta Morpugo. It was a cutout book simply subtitled: *A Book For Children*. In it, the pictures and verse about bugs, butterflies, and mice really came to life. That got me drawing—and writing."

Of course, Miss Spider is now a star with multimedia projects and toys in the works, but what's next and new for her creator? "Whatever I do next, I know I love making stories. The bookmaking process is a liberation for me from the years I toiled to produce handmade items. I think the life of a children's book author is bliss."

Kirk lives in the Finger Lakes region of New York with his wife Susan, his daughter Violet, two dogs, two fish, one iguana, and Teddy, the fluffiest hamster in the world.

Miss Spider's Guests

Who came to Miss Spider's tea party?

✏️ Color.

Bonus Box: Draw some insects that you can find outside on the back of this sheet.

©The Education Center, Inc. • *Spiders* • Preschool/Kindergarten • TEC3189

29

Counting All Bugs!

How many bugs do you see?

Count.

✏️ Write.

🖍️ Color.

✏️ Draw **5** rubber bugs with jolly mugs!

Buggy Fun Page

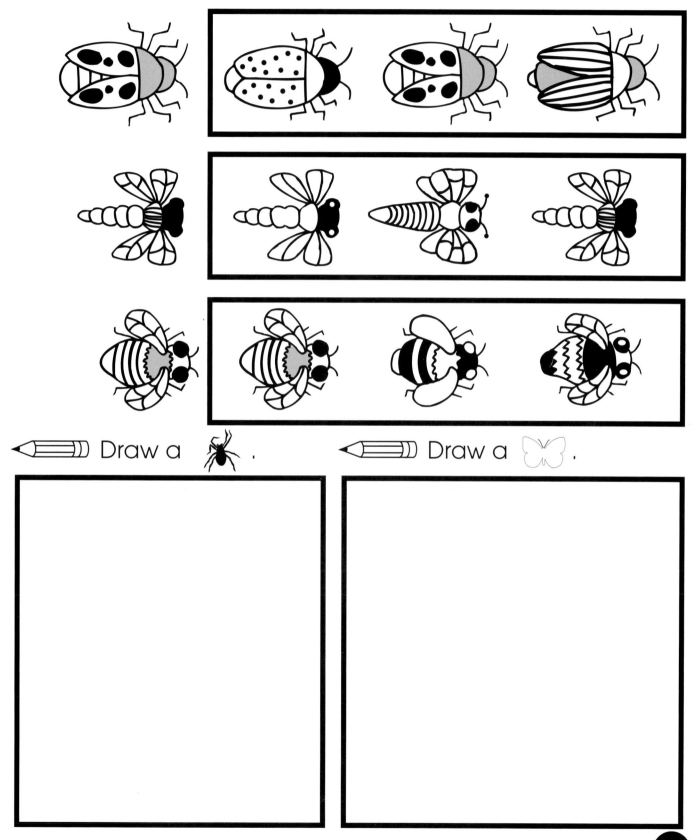

Color the matching bugs.

Draw a 🕷 .   Draw a 🦋 .

Note To The Teacher
Duplicate the book notes for each child as appropriate. Have each child color and cut out his book note. Encourage students to take their book notes home and share the story's content.

Book Notes

Miss Spider's Tea Party
by David Kirk
is a great counting book.

Ask me to name three different bugs found in the story.

Today I listened to a story about a spider. It was called

Miss Spider's Tea Party
by David Kirk.

Ask me to tell you about it.

.......Miss Spider's Tea Party......

Note To The Teacher
Duplicate this page several times on construction paper. Color the spiders; then laminate them and cut them out. Use a permanent marker to program the spiders with the matching skills of your choice. (For example, program half of the spiders with initial consonants and the other half with matching pictures.) To do this activity, a child matches each spider to a corresponding card.

Programmable Activity Cards

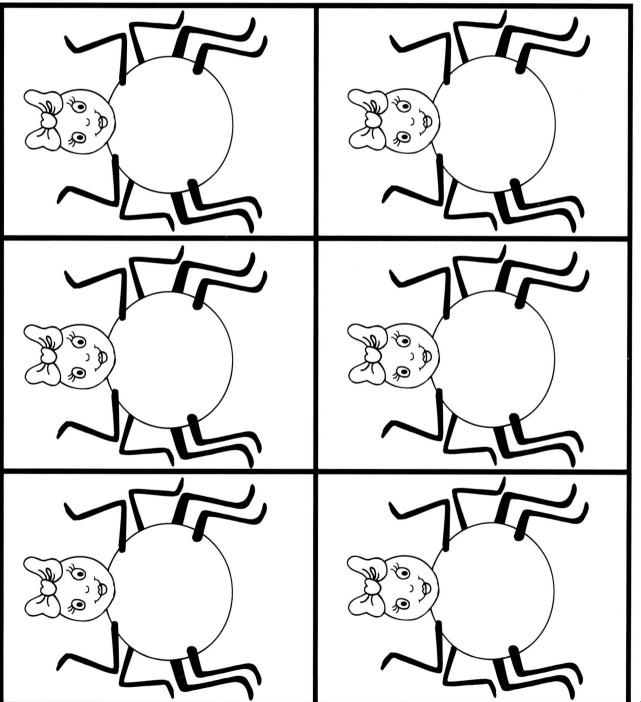

......Miss Spider's Tea Party......

How To Use Page 35

1. Duplicate the page for each child.
2. Place a classroom supply of cupcakes in a center with some white frosting, plastic knives, shoestring licorice pieces, and gumdrops.
3. After reviewing the recipe with your class, have each child visit the center and make a spider tea cake by following the steps in the recipe.
4. Students may enjoy eating their spider tea cakes while you reread *Miss Spider's Tea Party* or read another spider-related book.

Award

_____
Name

is spinning webs of good work!

Spider Tea Cakes

You will need:

 1 cupcake

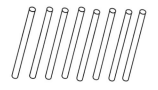 8 shoestring licorice pieces

white frosting

 1 gumdrop

1   Spread frosting on the cupcake.

2   Press the gumdrop in the frosting.

3   Add **8** shoestring licorice pieces.

......Spider Pop-Up Booklet......

How To Make A Spider Pop-Up Booklet
Pages 37, 38, And 39

Materials Needed For Each Student:

— one copy each of pages 37, 38, and 39 on white construction paper
— scissors
— crayons
— glue
— a pencil
— two wiggle eyes

1. Cut along the heavy solid lines on pages 37 and 38.
2. Fold the centerfold (pages 1 and 2) in half.
3. Glue the front booklet cover to the back of booklet page 1.
4. Glue the back booklet cover to the back of booklet page 2.
5. Color and cut out the spider body pattern on page 39; then glue it to the center of the front cover. Draw eight spider legs around the spider. To complete the front cover, glue wiggle eyes to the spider; then personalize the cover.
6. Color the pop-up spider pattern (page 39); then cut it out. See the illustration of the three-dimensional spider below. Fold your spider similarly. Then glue the end sections of the legs where indicated.
7. Read booklet page 1, and spider note A on page 39. Cut out the spider note labeled A and glue it where indicated on page 1. Write the numeral 8 inside the circle.
8. Read booklet page 2, and spider note B on page 39. Cut out the spider note labeled B and glue it where indicated on page 2. Draw an insect inside the circle.
9. Read the back cover of the booklet. Talk and read about spiders. Write some words to describe spiders.

Finished Sample

Spiders are

Back Cover

My Spider Book

by

Front Cover

37

Centerfold

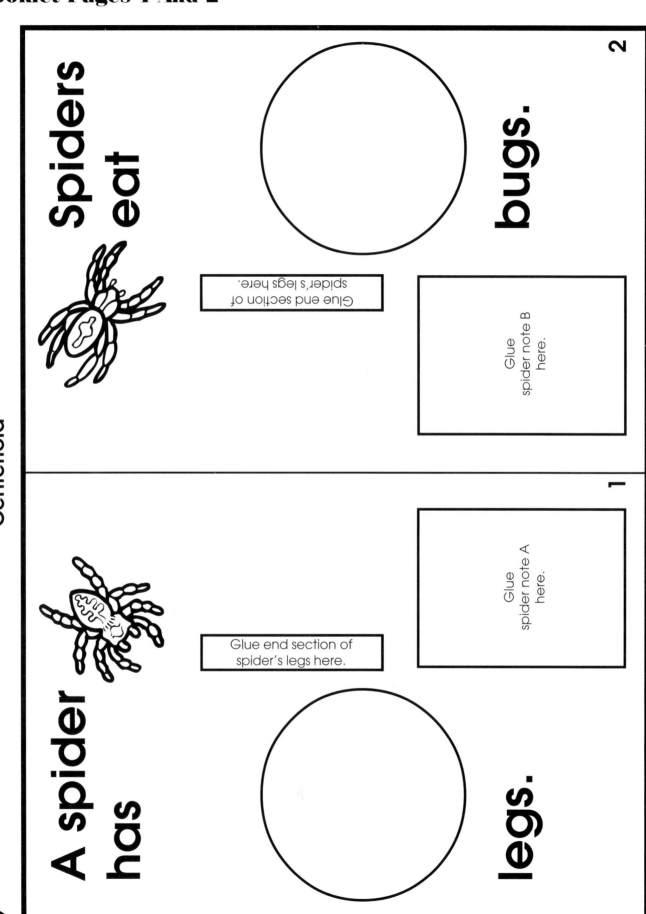

Spiders eat

bugs.

Glue end section of spider's legs here.

Glue spider note B here.

2

A spider has

legs.

Glue end section of spider's legs here.

Glue spider note A here.

1

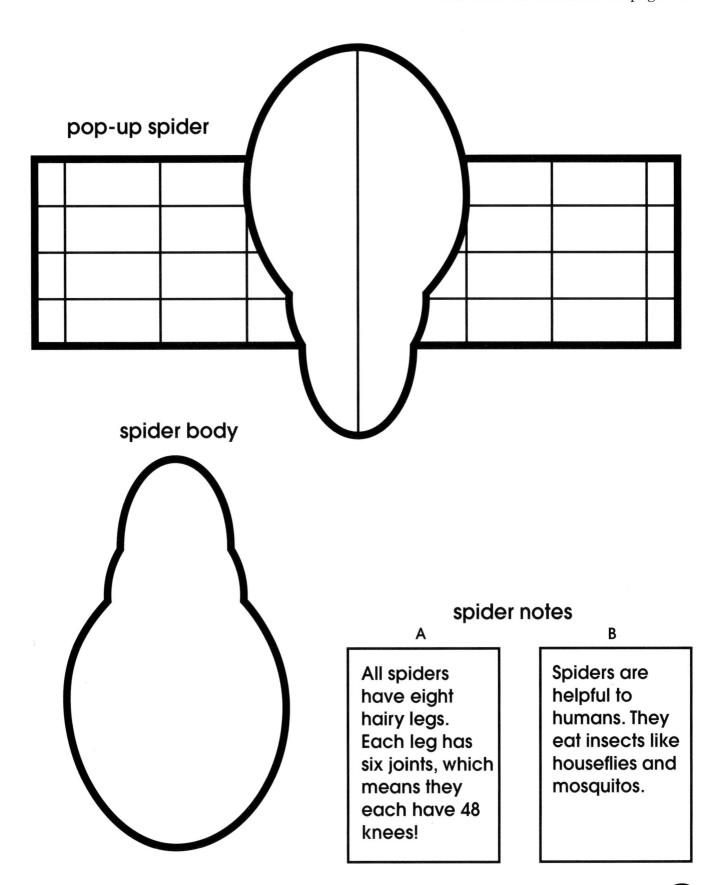

pop-up spider

spider body

spider notes

A

All spiders have eight hairy legs. Each leg has six joints, which means they each have 48 knees!

B

Spiders are helpful to humans. They eat insects like houseflies and mosquitos.

.........Spider Story Starter.........

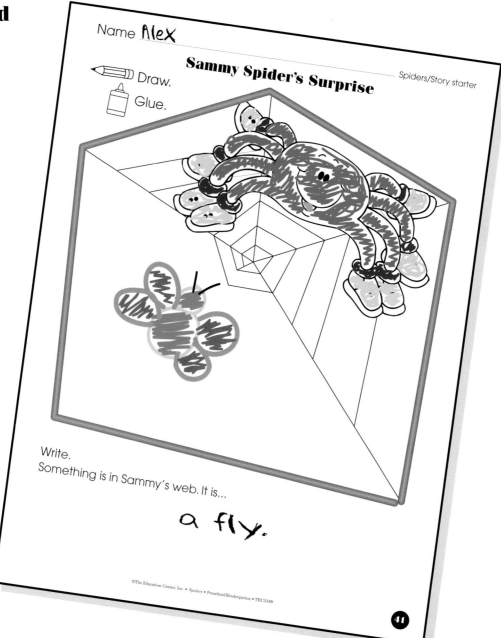

How To Use Page 41

1. Duplicate the page for each child.
2. Explain to your youngsters that some spiders catch their food in their webs. Have youngsters brainstorm what they would like to find in their webs if they were spiders. Have each child illustrate his ideas in the space provided.
3. Record each child's dictation at the bottom of the page.
4. Have each child color his page and glue yarn onto the dotted line around the spiderweb.

Materials Needed For Each Student:

—pencil
—crayons
—26-inch piece of yarn
—glue

Finished Sample

Name Alex

✏️ Draw.
🩹 Glue.

Sammy Spider's Surprise

Spiders/Story starter

Write.
Something is in Sammy's web. It is...

a fly.

Sammy Spider's Surprise

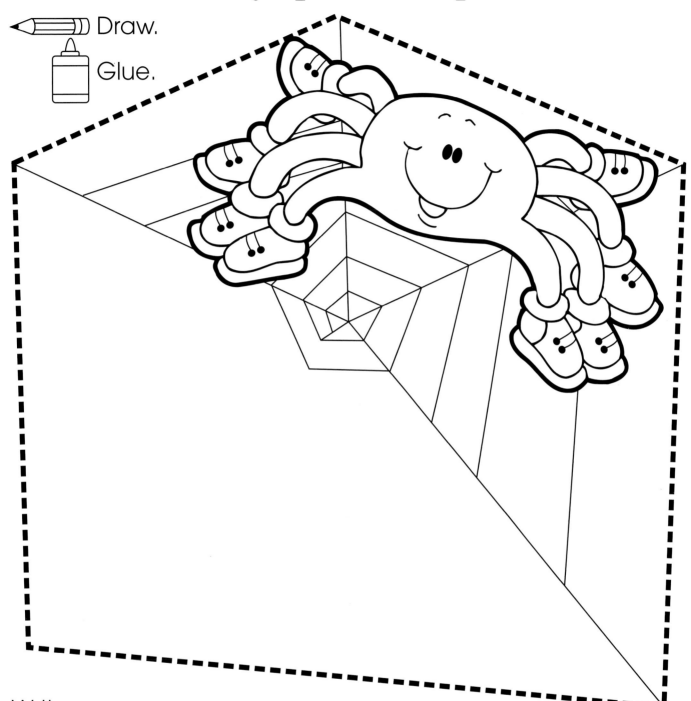

✏️ Draw.

🧴 Glue.

Write.

Something is in Sammy's web. It is…

Wooly's Web

Circle the matching letters.

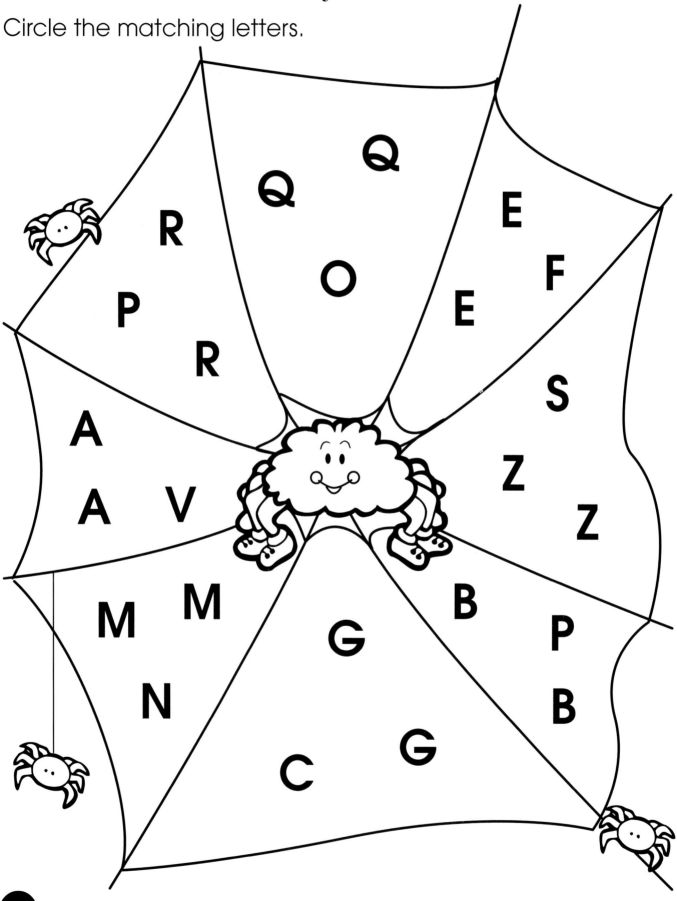

Spiffy Spiders

Color the matching letters.

Wee Webs

Color the matching letters.

Happy Hangers

Color the matching letters.

Name _____

Wacky Webwork

🖍 Color the matching shapes.

Note To The Teacher

Use this page to write a parent newsletter, an announcement, or an invitation. Then duplicate the page for each child.

Bookmarks

Take me to the library to look for a book about spiders!

Spider
Written by David Hawcock
Illustrated by Lee Montgomery
Published by Random House, Inc.

Amazing Spiders
Written by Alexandra Parsons
Photographed by Jerry Young
Published by Alfred A. Knopf, Inc.

The Itsy-Bitsy Spider
Retold & Illustrated by Iza Trapani
Published by Whispering Coyote
    Press, Inc.

The Spider
Written by Margaret Lane
Illustrated by Barbara Firth
Published by The Dial Press

The Roly Poly Spider
Written by Jill Sardegna
Illustrated by Tedd Arnold
Published by Scholastic Inc.

©The Education Center, Inc.

Take me to the library to look for a book about spiders!

Spider
Written by David Hawcock
Illustrated by Lee Montgomery
Published by Random House, Inc.

Amazing Spiders
Written by Alexandra Parsons
Photographed by Jerry Young
Published by Alfred A. Knopf, Inc.

The Itsy-Bitsy Spider
Retold & Illustrated by Iza Trapani
Published by Whispering Coyote
    Press, Inc.

The Spider
Written by Margaret Lane
Illustrated by Barbara Firth
Published by The Dial Press

The Roly Poly Spider
Written by Jill Sardegna
Illustrated by Tedd Arnold
Published by Scholastic Inc.

©The Education Center, Inc.